CHRIST:
THE PREEMINENT THRONE

AuthorHouse™
1663 Liberty Drive
Bloomington, IN 47403
www.authorhouse.com
Phone: 1-800-839-8640

Published by AuthorHouse   02/03/2012

ISBN: 978-1-4685-4928-7 (sc)
ISBN: 978-1-4685-4927-0 (e)

Library of Congress Control Number: 2012902095

CONTENTS

Dedication ....

Chapter 1.   Christ: The Preeminent Throne...

Chapter 2.   Pretender To The Throne ....

Chapter 3.   D'em Dry Bones ....

Chapter 4.   Satan's Seat-Hot Seat! ....

Chapter 5.   Adultery: Greener Grass ....

Chapter 6.   Fornication: Love The One You're With ....

Chapter 7.   High Chair Kissin' Cousins (Co-Sins) ....

Chapter 8.   Disruption, Division and Containment...

Chapter 9.   Self-Promotion / Self Aggrandizement...

Chapter 10. Conclusion...

Inspirational Bibliography...

DEDICATION

Rev. 4:2-

And immediately I was in the Spirit: and behold, a throne was set in heaven, and one sat on the throne. And He that sat was to look upon like a jasper and a sardine stone: and there was a rainbow round about the throne, in sight like unto an emerald . . . v. 5 and out of the throne proceeded lightnings and thunderings and voices: and there were seven lamps of fire burning before the throne, which are the seven spirits of God. And before the throne, there was a sea of glass like unto crystal.

Rev. 21:9 b

. . . saying, Come hither, I will show thee the Bride, the Lamb's wife. And he carried me away in the Spirit to a great and high mountain, and showed me that great city, the holy Jerusalem, descending out of heaven from God, having the glory of God; and her light was like unto a stone most precious, even like a jasper stone, clear as crystal.

SHE REFLECTS HER MAKER AND HER HUSBAND!

In loving memory of my Bigma, Mrs Lela Mae James, Little Mama, Mrs. Barbara Nell Nixon Bolden, Mr. (Apostle) Ed Kownacki, Sr., Papa Bill William Ross, Mrs. Nellie Crumbly, Ms. Emily Parker, Sister Lou, Ms. Daisy Williams, Mother Emma Cooper, Mr. Brooks, Mrs. Zenola Maxey, Ms. Catherine Gardner, Mother Carrie 'Christeen' Dawson.

Preeminent is dedicated to my dear husband, Pastor Bennie Cids Gardner, Sr., to my Presiding Bishops, Bishops Annie B. Campbell Pitre and Lonnie Pitre, Cousin Lee Mertis Harris, Dean Margaree Coleman Carter, CPA Cheryl Renee Cooper, Manager Maudie Warbington Ford, Social Worker Janet Warbington Williams, Mrs. Patsy Root, Mrs. Juanita Arterberry, Mrs Delores Blackford, Mrs Alice and Deborah Branson, Mrs. Sonja Reid, Mrs. Eulia Gray, Dr. Anjanette McFarland, Mrs. Gloria Grant, Mama Isophene Stewart and all of those who will love Christ at His appearing.

CHAPTER 1

CHRIST: THE PREEMINENT THRONE

The throne of Christ **is the preeminent throne.** The First and (with the) Last, I am He. Christ earned His right to sit far above all principalities, powers and any presumption of power that would ever exist in the earth, on the earth and above and beneath the earth. There are many contenders for the throne, but **only One who is worthy** and in authority:

Revelations 4:10-11:

> The four and twenty elders fall down before Him that sat on the throne, and worship Him that liveth forever and ever, and cast their crowns before the throne, saying, Thou art worthy, O Lord, to receive glory and honor and power: for Thou hast created all things, and **for Thy pleasure** they are and were created.

> And you hath He quickened, who were dead in trespasses and sins; But God who is rich in mercy for His GREAT LOVE wherewith He Loved US, Even when we were dead in sins, hath quickened us together with Christ, (by grace ye are saved) And hath raised us up together, and made us sit together in heavenly places in Christ Jesus. That in the ages to come, He might show the exceeding riches of His grace, in His kindness toward us, through Christ Jesus. Ephesians 2:1, 4-7.

He is the Alpha, The Omega, The Beginning and the End. The One who was, and is and is to come. He is the King of Kings and the Lord of Lords. There is no other name under heaven whereby men shall be saved. He is the Amen, the Faithful, and True.

Indeed, as it states in Psalms 118:22:

> The stone which the builders rejected has become the headstone of the corner. This is the Lord's doing, it is marvelous in our eyes. This is the day that the Lord hath made we will rejoice and be glad in it.

As stated in the prophet Jeremiah chapter 17 verse 12 et seq.:

> A glorious high throne from the beginning is the place of our sanctuary. O Lord, the hope of Israel, all who forsake You shall be ashamed. Those who depart from Me shall be written in the earth, because they have forsaken the **Lord**, the fountain of living waters. Heal me, O Lord, and I shall be healed; save me, and I shall be saved, for You are my praise. Indeed they say to me, where is the word of the Lord? Let it come now! As for me, I have not hurried away from being a shepherd who follows You, Nor have I desired the woeful day; You know what came out of my lips; It was right there before You, do not be a terror to me; You are my hope in the day of doom.

Revelations chapter 19: 11-16 makes it abundantly clear why Jeremiah was in anguish. He knew that the great and awesome Day of the Lord would come. He fully expected that at this coming, if not before, he would be vindicated:

> Then I saw heaven opened, and behold, a white horse. And He who sat on him was called Faithful and True, and in righteousness He judges and makes war. His eyes were like a flame of fire, and on His head were many crowns. He had a name written that no one knew except Himself. *He was clothed in a robe dipped in blood, and his name is called*

> *The Word of God.*

> *And the armies in heaven, clothed in fine linen, white and clean, followed him on white horses. Now out of His mouth goes a sharp sword, that with it He should strike the nations. And He Himself will rule them with a rod of iron. He Himself treads the wine press of the fierceness of the wrath of Almighty God. And He has on His robe and on His thigh a name written:*

> *King of Kings and the Lord of Lords.*

Jeremiah said that cursed is the man who trusts in man. He also said that cursed is the man who departs from the Lord and makes flesh his strength. Jeremiah 17:5,6;Psalms 118. He further iterated, that such a person would be parched, shriveled up, and dried. Blessed, on the other hand, would be the man who trusts in the Lord. Such a person would flourish like a tree planted by a river of living waters as stated in Psalms 1. Jeremiah 17:7-8. That's why he referred to God as the Fountain of Living Waters. Jeremiah exhausted himself, and practically summoned his own death, trying to turn the people's hearts back to their God.

Revelations truly reveals the dire consequences of departing from the only true God:

And I saw a great white throne, and Him that sat on it, from whose face the earth and heaven fled away; and there was found no place for them. Revelations 20:11. And He that sat upon the throne said, Behold I make all things new. And He said unto me Write, for these words are true and faithful. And He said unto me "It is done!". I am the Alpha and Omega, the beginning and the end. Revelations 21:5-6a.

Despite the beauty of the coming King, the scene invokes terror. Isaiah 63 is striking in its description of the coming wrath. This is no longer Mary's little lamb, the babe in the manger, the one wrapped in swaddling clothes. This is the King, the Lion of the tribe of Judah:

Why is your apparel red, and Your garments like one who treads in the wine press? I have trodden the wine press alone, and from the peoples no one was with Me. For I have trodden them in My anger, and trampled them in My fury; their blood is sprinkled upon My garments, and I have stained all My robes. For the day of vengeance is in My heart, and the year of My redeemed has come. I looked, but there was no one to help, and I wondered that there was no one to up hold; therefore My own arm brought salvation for Me; and My own fury, it sustained Me. I have trodden down the peoples in My anger, made them drunk in My fury, and brought down their strength to the earth.

That our Savior is about to handle His business is a fact. Sinners better get ready for that great day. Although God is tarrying, it should not be taken as a sign that He is not coming at all. Oh no, His return is definite and destructive. No doubt about it. It will be a new day. Who shall be able to stand?!

On the cross He cried, It is finished! Now He will cry, It is done. As it is stated in Isaiah 22:20:

> Then it shall be in that day, that I will call My servant Eliakim the son of Hilkiah; I will clothe him with your robe and strengthen him with your belt; I will commit your responsibility into his hand, He shall be a father to the inhabitants of Jerusalem and to the house of Judah. The key of the house of David I will lay on his shoulder; so He shall open and no one shall shut; and He shall shut, and no one shall open. I will fasten him as a peg in a secure place, and he will become a glorious throne to his father's house. They will hang on him all the glory of his father's house, the offspring and the issue, all vessels of small quantity, from the cups to all the pitchers. In that day, says the Lord of Hosts, the peg that is fastened in the secure place will be removed and be cut down and fall, and the burden that was on it will be cut off, for the Lord has spoken.

Though the former paragraph references Eliakim, of a truth, it is identical to the events of the first coming of Christ. This first coming was to secure our pardon and deliverance from bondage to satan and sin. We have been washed, we have been sanctified. There is no more deliverance from sin. Christ, once offered was, and still is, a full, perfect and sufficient sacrifice—an atonement and propitiation for our sins.

Christ is sitting at the right hand of the Majesty from on High. From thence He shall come to judge the quick and the dead. It behooves us, therefore, neither to trifle with Him or His authority. As the scripture states, what shall we say then, shall we continue in sin that grace may abound, God forbid! Romans 6:1.

To this end, God gave me two very sure and distinct words which ought to characterize what we as the saints of God are about in these last and final days. The one word is "metanoia" and the other is "parousia".

"Metanoia" is defined in the Hebrew Greek Key Study Bible by Spiros Zodhiates and AMG International, Inc. 1984, as a change of mind, repentance, to repent. It is a change or alteration of mind Hebrews 12:17. Repentance, a change of mind from evil to good or from worse to better. Matthew 3: 11, 9:13; Acts 20:21.

"Nous" in the New Testament is mind, the faculty of moral reflection. When combined with "aphesis", which denotes remission of sins, and identifies the change as being concrete and sincere as opposed to mere fear of the consequences of the sin. Change resulting from fear of the consequences is never permanent. Rather, the change succumbs once the anticipation or apprehension of fear of repercussions is removed.

The bottom line is that God is looking for a change of heart, as Peter stated not just my hands but my head also. John 13. People laugh about Peter saying that.

However, Peter recognized, as Paul said, in his flesh doth no good thing dwell. Hence, he wanted his hands washed because he knew that he had the tendency to defile them. This is evident by his subsequent rage and cutting off of the high priest's servant's ear.

Peter knew, that despite his glowing Holy Ghost inspired declaration of who Christ was, that his head required some adjustments. He did not have the mind of Christ. Thus we see Peter being rebuked for telling Christ that he would not suffer Him to die on the cross. We see Peter warming himself at the enemy's fire while Christ is being prepared to stand trial. We see Peter preparing to go fishing and inviting the others to join him in John 21 assuming that the Savior is no more.

"Parousia" means presence, being present, a coming to a place, near, to be at hand. It is connected to the Second Coming of Christ.

The gist of what our Heavenly Father is commanding us, is to get our house in order, to clean up our acts, that is "metanoia", and to prepare to meet our Maker, which is "parousia". It cannot get any simpler or direct than that. These two points warrant no clarification, just obedience.

CHAPTER 2

PRETENDER TO THE THRONE

satan could very well be the lead vocalist in the song I Am The Great Pretender, by the Platters. He unsuccessfully engineered a coup d'état. He sought to unseat Jehovah Saboath and to make himself the Royal personage. What a faux pas—big mistake!

In Isaiah 14 we see this tragic flight of fancy unfold. He was not satisfied to be the preeminent archangel, he decided to contend for the throne. As the preeminent angel, Lucifer really had it going on. He was all that:

You were the seal of perfection, full of wisdom and perfect in beauty. You were in Eden, the garden of God; every precious stone was your covering; the sardius, the topaz and the diamond, beryl, onyx, and jasper, sapphire, turquoise, and emerald with gold. The workmanship of your timbrels and pipes was prepared for you on the day you were created. You were the anointed cherub who covers; I established you; You were on the holy mountain of God; You walked back and forth in the midst of fiery stones. You were perfect in your ways from the day you were created, Till iniquity was found in you. By the abundance of your trading you became filled with violence within, and you sinned; therefore I cast you as a profane thing out of the mountain of God; and I destroyed you O covering cherub from the midst of the fiery stones. Your heart was lifted up because of your beauty; you corrupted your wisdom for the sake of your splendor; I cast you to the ground, I laid you before kings that they might gaze at you. Ezekiel 28:12-17.

Imagine that, satan, in his former state as Lucifer, was deemed perfect. Everything referenced in Genesis was 'and God saw that it was good', so Lucifer was obviously a 'cut above' from his inception!

Lucifer had wisdom, the main characteristic of Christ (Proverbs 8 and I wisdom dwelt with Him from the beginning) (Isaiah 11:1) and he was handsome.

Prior to his demise, we are told that he was even in the garden of Eden, a place of pure perfection. And, he was on the mount of God! Right there.

Not only was he uncommonly musically inclined, which leads one to believe he delighted God with his talents, he was adorned with the very stones that reflect the breastplate, the Urim and Thummim ie., the lights and perfections (Exodus 28:30; Numbers 27:21),the throne, the bride, and the walls of the holy city, New Jerusalem.

In addition, his wardrobe included gold, the substance of the streets of the holy city. Revelations 21:18-21. Adorned like this, God must have considered him sufficiently trustworthy to reflect the essence of his relationship with men and creation, including the holy city. Thus, the depths of the betrayal become manifest. To be entrusted with so much and to trifle with it is unpardonable, even though it did not take God by surprise.

Only the priests could utilize the Urim and the Thummim to inquire of God. It was the most sacred artifact. For Lucifer to even have the semblance or reflection of such a sacred trust is not only fascinating, but mind boggling. It leads to the inference that he may have even been privy to the early consults. After all, are they not all ministering spirits sent forth to minister unto those that shall be the heirs of salvation. Such regal splendor cannot be found in any other creation. Solomon in all his glory was not arrayed like Lucifer. Indeed, God showed out when He made Lucifer. What an ingrate!!! Ah! The mystery of ungodliness!

It gets even deeper. When you look at the description of him walking in the midst of the fiery stones, one might presume that he was present, and perhaps in some measure a part of the sacrificial offerings. Additionally, when you think of him as the anointed cherub that covers, the cherubs covered the mercy seat on the Ark of the Covenant. Maybe he was also involved in coverage of the throne in some respect although God certainly does not need an armorbearer!

It is safe to state that Lucifer was in 'the Situation Room'. More specifically, Lucifer was around the throne in the presence of the Most High God, where mercy was dispensed. Ezekiel 28 states plainly that he was on the mount of God. Lucifer in—the—house! Hey!!! See Ezekiel 20:40; Exodus 25:17-22; 37:1-9.

Ezekiel 28 specifies the main count of the indictment against Lucifer. It was his trading. His transactions, his dealings with Mammon and consequent wealth, filled him with violence. His heart was lifted up and he sinned. Ezekiel 28:16-17. 'How art thou fallen indeed!' Isaiah 14.

So we redirect our footsteps to Isaiah 14 where the usurpation is underway. In verses 9 through 11, God gives the specifics of the punishment that He promised Lucifer in Ezekiel 28. He stated that he would lay him out before kings and that they would gaze at him in horror and glee.

In Isaiah chapter 14 God indicates that He not only stirred up the kings of the earth, He also raised up the dead who once occupied thrones. "All the chief ones of the earth; It has raised up from their thrones". This makes Thriller by Michael Jackson a less grand cemetery ballroom affair.

Apparently both living and dead monarchs would address Lucifer in the midst of his fall. They are relishing the fact that he had become weak. His pomp was a thing of the past. Maggots and worms replaced the magnificent jewels with which he was once adorned. Nebuchadrezzar with claws and talons crawling on all fours was less ominous in his dementia.

In Isaiah 14:12, it is stated that satan weakened the nations. This was apparently accomplished through the trading that ultimately caused him to sin. Ezekiel 28. He already had concourse in heaven, as well as apparent access to the throne. Yet, in verse 13, he said in his heart I will ascend into heaven. No doubt this indicates an intrusion by force as opposed to his normal position as the covering cherub. We see why Peter prophesies, 'Thou art the Christ, the Son of the Living God. Upon this rock I will build my church **and the gates of hell shall not prevail against it . . .'** satan's plans were foreknown.

Next satan proclaims that "he will exalt his throne above the stars of God." Not content to be the seal of perfection, he now wants to Lord it over all of the other angels. It was not enough that he bore the reflection of the New Jerusalem, the breastplate, had concourse in the offerings, the communications and around the throne. No! He would have it all. He's going to control the stars. Stars refers to the angels (see Revelations 1) Maybe he will be over some of those stars in Hollywood, and certainly the one-third that God gave pink slips with him, but that's all. To let him know who was in charge, God marked the birthplace of the Savior by requiring that we follow the True Star. Matthew 2:2, 9.

That certainly was some serious star/angel/dust satan was smoking. His next claim is 'to sit on the mount of the congregation, on the farthest side of the north'. Maybe this is the origin of drug testing! Some people get dizzy when they get too high. Psalms 48:1-2:

> Great is the Lord, and greatly to be praised in the city of our God, and His holy mountain. Beautiful in elevation, the joy of the whole earth, is Mount Zion on the sides of the North, the city of the great King.

And again in Psalms 87:1:

> His foundation is in the holy mountains. The Lord loves the gates of Zion more than all the dwellings of Jacob. Glorious things are spoken of you, O city of God.

These verses are cited to substantiate that satan knew exactly what it was that he was saying in his heart. **Zion was (and is) God's place**. As stated herein above, the holy city was on the mount, was greatly to be praised, was beautiful and the joy of the whole earth.

No doubt, satan saw the glory that only belongs to the Most High God. This is also seen in Psalms 46:4: There is a river whose streams shall make glad the city of God, the holy place of the tabernacle of the Most High. The streams were once referenced as rivers in Eden in Genesis 2:11-14. They are also referenced as rivers in Ezekiel 47:1-12. The river around the throne is seen as well in Revelations 21-22.

Again, not content to be in the Big-League, he had to be the big cheese. Now, satan is just a quesadilla. The final blow, of course, was when satan could bear it no longer to dance around the edge of the plate. His ego necessitated an outright declaration of his intentions. In Isaiah 14:14 : "I will ascend above the heights of the clouds, **I will be like the Most High**." That's all she wrote. Destination hell was no longer a possibility, it was certain.

Really, how dumb can you get? To put this into perspective imagine the executive secretary or first assistant to the boss. Such a personage is privy to all of the 'goings on' in the camp. All that that individual is not told or instructed, she is in a position to discover by virtue of company memo or gossip. Even when they are not 'in the know' on a given issue, those who are will share what they know with this secretary or assistant in order to curry favor for later. Now, it just defies the imagination that such a person so close to the One who is in charge would make such a deliberate blunder and seek to usurp His authority. Yet, that is exactly what satan attempted.

That every transgression is met with a recompense of reward is evident in the swift punishment meted out to satan. God promised him in Ezekiel 28 that He would put him on display. That the dead as well as the living would see him in his demotion. God is true to His word. Truly, every promise of God is yeah and amen. In Isaiah 14:15-19 satan is described as being brought down to the depths of the pit, cast out of his grave like an abominable branch, while all of the kings of the nations are in sweet repose in their graves. It's pretty bad when your cronies fare better than you do.

satan's conduct is referred to in II Thessalonians 2 as the 'mystery of lawlessness.' In verse four it **states the man of sin, the son of perdition, who opposes and exalts himself above all that is called God or that is worshiped, so that he sits as God in the temple of God, showing himself that he is God**. What a deception?! Showing himself is correct, everyone else knows better!

In II Thessalonians 2: 9 it is stated that the coming of the lawless one is according to the working of satan, with all power, signs, and lying wonders, and with all unrighteous deception among those who perish, because they did not receive the love of the truth, that they might be saved.

satan is truly the author of 'if that first you don't succeed try try again.' Not content with having duped woman, who handed the curse over to Adam, satan proceeds to unsuccessfully attempt to undermine The Son of God Himself. The very things that he used in verses 9-10 of II Thessalonians, he already tried and failed against the Christ in Luke chapter 4.

The power, signs, lying wonders, and unrighteous deception are quite pronounced in the challenge to Christ. He was enticed to abuse his authority by turning the stones into bread, with satan offering Him the kingdoms of the world in exchange for worship (Luke 4:7). When Christ refused, satan attempted to get Him to commit suicide by throwing Himself down from the pinnacle of the temple.

Remember, this was just after the baptism of Christ by John the Baptist. The sky opened, the Spirit descended upon Christ like a dove, and our Heavenly Father spoke 'this is My Beloved Son in Whom I am well pleased.' satan, obviously an uninvited guest at this event, as he was in Job's time, when God called his sons together and satan was in the midst, came bearing strange gifts indeed. He is the kind of babysitter you certainly don't want to accidentally hire. He is like the jealous mother of the cheerleader who will kill your starstudded child at the first opportunity.

satan just couldn't stand the thought, that God would still allow His creation to stand after the betrayal in the garden of Eden. Patently aware that his days were numbered once the Christ child was planted in Mary's womb, he sought through Herod's efforts to dupe the magi, and here on his own, to undo Him before He can succeed in redeeming mankind.

On a more mundane level, have you ever had anyone either in your employ, in your household, in your friends' circle, in your family, church, profession, civic group that just stayed on your heels, breathed down your neck, followed, watched, mimicked your every move? They smiled in your face, as the old O-Jays song says, all the time trying to take your place, the backstabbers! satan, on the other hand, is unabashed. He is up front, in yo' face and personal about his supplanting.

CHAPTER 3

D'EM DRY BONES

The Bible speaks of 'thrones of iniquity' in Psalms 94:20. It is talking about those who devise evil by utilization of their legal authority. However, thrones of iniquity, is also an apt description of all those iconic things that we set up in our lives.

Character is built by conduct. It is not built by what one says that they are. If it were that easy we'd all be happy campers. Unfortunately, or perhaps fortunately, depending on your perspective, the same can be said about thrones. More specifically, what absorbs your time? What are you consumed with? What is most important to you? What do you give precedence? What keeps you awake at night? What is your lifeblood or what makes your heart skip a beat or better yet what grabs your immediate attention . . . ? Whatever or whoever that may be, they occupy a central preeminent position in your life whether you admit it or not. That place is a **THRONE**. So let's take a look at what satan has used to draw, **entice and seduce you away from Almighty God.**

Whatever or whoever sits on the throne of your heart in lieu of Jehovah Nisi, Jehovah Rapha, Jehovah Rophe, Jehovah Shalom, the Dayspring from on High, Elohim, El Gibor, El Ellyon, Jehovah Tsidkenu, Jehovah Rohe, Emmanuel, El Shaddai, Jehovah Makkedesh, The Fountain of Living Waters, the Lamb of God—is bone desert dry in comparison.

As God stated in his indictment against Israel, they have chosen for themselves hewn cisterns that can hold no water! Jeremiah 2:13.

In the next several chapters, we will be looking at these thrones:

Galatians 5:16-21:

Now the works of the flesh are evident, which are: adultery, fornication, uncleanness, licentiousness, idolatry, sorcery, hatred, contentions, jealousies, outbursts of wrath, selfish ambitions, dissensions, heresies, envy, murders, drunkenness, revelries, and the like; of which I tell you before hand, just as I told you in times past, ***that those who practice such things will not inherit the kingdom of God.***

Romans 1:26-32:

For this reason God gave them up to vile passions. For even their women exchanged the natural use for what is against nature. Likewise also the men, leaving the natural use of the woman, burned in their lust for one another, men with men committing what is shameful, and receiving in themselves the penalty of their error which was due. And they did not like to retain God in their knowledge, God gave them over to a debased mind, to do those things which are not fitting; being filled with all unrighteousness, sexual immorality, wickedness, covetousness, maliciousness, full of envy, murder, strife, deceit, evil mindedness, they are whisperers, backbiters, haters of God, violent, proud, boasters, inventors of evil things, disobedient to parents, undiscerning, untrustworthy, unloving, unforgiving, unmerciful; and who ***knowing the righteous judgment of God, that those who practice such things are worthy of death, not only do the same but also approve of those who practice them.***

Revelations 22:15:

But outside are dogs and sorcerers and the sexually immoral and murderers and the idolaters, and whoever loves and practices a lie.

I am persuaded (Romans 8:28 et seq) that not only dry bones can live (Ezekiel 37), but dry thrones can be dismantled and replaced with The True and Living God, the FOUNTAIN OF LIVING WATERS!

P. S. I can hear you now, I don't do those things. Oh no, not I, it is Christ that lives in me! Yet, Christ said and such were some of you that ye have been washed, ye have been sanctified . . . so, indulge me, and take a stroll down memory lane. Why?! So you won't be so self-righteous the next time you run into your old creation with someone else's face on it! In other words, don't get 'too new' that God cannot use you!

Christ said all of our righteousness is as a filthy rag, a menstrous cloth. Isaiah 64. Finally, He cautions that the self-righteous are a smoke in His nostrils.

If any of this is still you, just holler 'help me Jesus.'

If none of this is you, shout: 'He is still a miracle worker'!!!

If it is you, have faith in God. Rome was not built in a day, and it may take a while to lay your foundation and build you upright so do not despair. As Paul stated in I Corinthians 13:12: but for now we see through a glass, darkly; but then face to face: now I know in part; but then shall I know even as also I am known.

The bottom line is you are growing. Thank the Lord. That is why it is called "moving from glory to glory": II Corinthians 3:17-18:

Now the Lord is the Spirit; and where the Spirit of the Lord is, there is liberty. But we all, with unveiled face, beholding as in a mirror the glory of the Lord, are being transformed into the same image from glory to glory, just as by the Spirit of the Lord. (And when it is all said and done, the glory will be restored to its RIGHTFUL OWNER—Rev. 4)

YOU Are Going To Make It! As Paul stated in II Corinthians 4: 16-18:

Therefore we do not lose heart. Even though our outward man is perishing, yet the inward man is being renewed day by day. For our light affliction, which is but for a moment, is working for us a far more exceeding and eternal weight of glory, while we do not look at the things which are seen, but at the things which are not seen. For the things which are seen are temporary, but the things which are not seen are eternal.

Isaiah 64:8: But Now, Oh Lord, You are Our Father. We are the clay and You, Our Potter, and all we are the work of Your hands.

However, this word still rings true. Galatians 5:1: Stand fast therefore in the liberty wherewith Christ hath made us free, and be not entangled again in a yoke of bondage.

Once free, make every effort to stay free! Hallelujah! Fasten your seat belt.

CHAPTER 4

SATAN'S SEAT-HOT SEAT!

And to the angel of the church in Pergamos write, these things says He who has the sharp two edged sword:

I know your works, and where you dwell, where Satan's throne is. And you hold fast to My name, and did not deny My faith even in the days in which Antipas, was My faithful martyr, who was killed among you, where satan dwells. But I have a few things against you, because you have there those who hold the doctrine of Balaam, who taught Balak to put a stumbling block before the children of Israel, to eat things sacrificed to idols, and to commit sexual immorality. Thus you also have those who hold the doctrine of the Nicolaitans, which thing I hate. Repent, or else I will come to you quickly and will fight against them with the sword of My mouth. He who has an ear let Him hear what the Spirit says to the churches. To him who overcomes I will give some of the hidden manna to eat. And I will give him a white stone, and on the stone a new name written which no one knows except him who receives it. Revelations 2:12-18.

Interesting. Satan had his own little citadel. What is a babay's (sic) highchair to the throne of the Most High? Really now! Apparently, Pergamum was on the edge of a cliff crowning a steep hill 1000 feet above the plane. There was an immense altar there dedicated to Zeus the Greek god.

Quite frankly, all of this adds up when you consider that in Luke 4 Jesus was taken to the pinnacle of the temple where satan said to Him that all of this will be Yours if You will only worship me. Evidently he thought he had something to offer the King of Kings and the Lord of Lords, a hot seat.

No doubt a great pretender will not be thwarted by the failure to have the actual. You have to give him credit for being desperate and utilizing it as a creative catalyst in establishing his own 'wannabe' little regime.

In the lexical aids to the New Testament Key Hebrew Greek Study Bible satan's name is derived from the Aramaic and simply means adversary. A more apt description would be copycat. He is the prince of the devils and therefore bears the other name "diabolos". It is descriptive of one who stands, posits or casts or thrusts himself between two in order to separate them. He could readily be called the schematic, the schism or what he is best at parlaying, division.

The other appellation is that of "false accuser" as well as the "prince of the fallen angels." None of this is shocking when you consider that he accused Job of only serving God for the 'goodies'. Job 1-2. In Isaiah 14 satan's entire goal was to supplant the Most High God with full expectation of being over all of creation as well as the Heavenly Host. That failing he established his little fiefdom in lieu of Zeus, at best a cheap imitation of a god who was no god, exchanging a myth (Zeus) for a myth (himself).

Obviously satan's seat is wherever sin is, that's why he is known as the prince of the devils. You can be certain that wherever a sin is, there is at least one devil/demon assigned to it. He does delegate. How quaint. satan is chief trash collector (no offense to the profession). His demons are the tares and the chaff.

This is why sin is so enticing, so endearing, so difficult to extricate oneself from. When you consider that satan's lust for God's authority was so intense, that his desire was so tremendously fanciful, so delectably described, it is not shocking that the sins that he concocts for unwitting souls to fall prey to are equally damnable.

Recall that in the description of the terminology, it indicates that satan is divisive, that he casts himself in the midst of and divides. We have a very distinct example of that here. God is saying to Pergamos, that although they have held on to His name as well as the faith, satan still has a stronghold there. In fact his web(site) (pun intended) is so intense that one of God's most faithful servants, Antipas, lost his life as a result of it.

Do not take this lightly. The Christians at Pergamos had works which were evidently within God's purview and apparently to His satisfaction at some point. They also had God's name, the Name that is above every other name, the Name unto which every knee shall bow and every tongue confess, the only Name whereby men shall be saved, THAT NAME!

Third, they held onto the faith. What a formula. Without faith it is impossible to please Him. Now faith is the substance of things hoped for the evidence of things not yet seen. He that comes to God must believe that He is and that He is a rewarder of those that diligently seek Him . . . so how can it possibly be that satan was able to establish a throne in the midst of all this 'Godness' going on? It is baffling. It defies the imagination. It creates quite the mental as well as spiritual dilemma for anyone who has undertaken to love and to worship God. It seemed that Pergamos had what it took to succeed in the spirit.

Perhaps verse 14 provides the illumination that we are seeking. Pergamos had all of its ducks in a row, but unwittingly opened the trap door for the Wolf. That Pergamos overstepped its bounds is evident from the fact that God said that He had a few things against it. One was that it had undertaken to curse that which God blessed. We are instructed to bless our enemies and curse them not. In doing to the contrary, holding the doctrine of Balaam, they added to the word of God. It seems that they cast stumbling blocks as well which may explain how Antipas became ensnared and martyred.

Additionally, God says that they taught others to eat things sacrificed to idols. Now Paul informs us that things sacrificed to idols are nothing if we unwittingly eat them and give thanks. It may very well be that they openly sacrificed to idols and ate their delicacies. Would that they had taken lessons from Daniel declining to defile himself with the King's dainties.

The next thing that God indicts them for is committing fornication. As we learn in the next chapter, our bodies are the Temple of Christ and not our own. We are to glorify God in our bodies. It seems that they furthered the transgression by holding to the doctrine of the Nicolaitans, which thing God said He hates. It was no small snare when you consider that the church of Ephesus had the same issue, although it had works, labor, patience, intolerance of evil and keen spiritual discernment. They held on, they labored in patience and did not faint but left their FIRST LOVE! (Revelations 1:4)

Further research on the doctrine of the Nicolaitans reveals that it was a gnostic sect, 'ergon'. It was not just a theory or belief. No, it was a work, employment, an accumulated and continuous endeavor, calling, occupation or sacrifice making manifest who a person is and what they are made of ie., disclosing character.

Similar to Balaam and Jezebel, the Nicolaitans wing it. They taught that it was okay to eat things offered to idols, that committing fornication was not sinful, there was no such thing as adultery since they taught that it was okay to have a community of wives or a harem in modern-day parlance. If you can have all you want, when you want, with whosoever will, then nothing is 'out of bounds'!?

Taking all of this into perspective, it is readily apparent why Antipas was martyred. He probably spoke against the foregoing conduct as a vehemently as Ezra, Nehemiah, Isaiah and Jeremiah lamented the harlotry of Israel and Judah. Denouncing their orgies was as sure a prelude to a sentence of death as John the Baptist's denunciation of the relationship between Herod and his sister-in-law. Defying some 'thrones', those that are tenuous at best in the first place, can be deadly.

All things considered, God was pretty generous in even allowing them the opportunity to repent. Particularly frightening is the threat (promise) to fight against them with the sword of His mouth should they not quickly repent. Since God's Word shall not return unto Him void but accomplish that which He sent it to do, Isaiah 55, this is no idle threat. In fact, in Psalms 12 his word has been purified in the furnace of earth seven times. HIS word is Logos, His Only Begotten

Son. We already know that His checks cash at the bank, Golgotha Hill Bank and Trust at Calvary.

More astounding of course is the promise of His mercy. To the one that overcomes, and we know that the victory that overcomes is even our faith, He promises to give of the hidden manna. Now, this is intriguing. Moses gave the manna in the wilderness and they died. Christ is the bread of life (John5-6), and he that eats of Him shall never hunger. (Isaiah 55). So it is somewhat surprising, that He will give the ones that are penitent part of Himself. This is obviously a complete pardon and full restoration for prior misconduct.

As a further blessing, those who repent and therefore overcome, are promised the white stone, clearly depicting that the memory or taint of the sin, the rebellion is purged, the slate is clean, all is forgiven. A white stone from the great white throne of Revelations (Revelations 20:11).

A new name is bestowed upon the one who successfully extricates himself from the fleshpot heresy. There will no longer be any remembrance of past heretical involvement.

Research of the new name, the word is 'Onoma', indicates that it helps you to know a thing or accurately portray you. It can also represent the description of the character of the individual, the name, the reputation, implied dignity or authority or the substitute or representative of a person. Clearly this indicates that the individual who gets the new name will be known as a representative of Christ (who will also have a name that is not known) as well as having delegated authority. As stated in John 14:13: whatsoever ye shall ask in My name that will I do, that is whatever conforms to the character of Christ as well as His purpose.

Again and again and again, once sin is set aside, restoration to the family is so complete, that it is as though one had never left, quite like the prodigal son. No longer a rejected stone, as Christ had been. The scepter of mercy is constantly extended as when Esther went before the king—without that scepter, which Christ is, we die!

Now that we have established that satan has a seat where sin runs rampant, we should become patently aware how deep our submission to his inducements sifts away at our very being as Christians and undermines the throne of the true King, Jesus Christ our Lord and our Savior, in our hearts. Lord I want to be a Christian in my HEART!

CHAPTER 5

ADULTERY: GREENER GRASS

There is truly something to be said about the Green Green grass of home! According to our cows and horses, the grass is greener on the other side. How would they know they're dumb animals? We should know better!

I have been crucified with Christ, it is no longer I who live, but Christ Lives in Me, and the Life Which I now live in the flesh I live by faith in the Son of God, *Who loved me and Gave Himself for me*. Galatians 2: 20.

HISTORICAL PERSPECTIVE

There is no truer picture of the damage that can be caused by adultery than incidences involving Abraham, David, Potiphar's wife after Joseph, and the numerous political incidents that we have witnessed in the last decade. The worst of the worst is the one depicted in Hosea. He reflects the Lord, patiently reeling in his errant wife, Gomer or Israel.

Paul tells us in I Corinthians 7 that a husband and wife (as designed by God) are to avoid adultery, by letting every man have his own wife, and letting every woman have her own husband. Then Paul states, let the husband render unto the wife due benevolence: and likewise also the wife unto the husband. The wife hath not power of her own body, but the husband: and likewise also the husband hath not power of his own body, but the wife. Defraud ye not one the other, except it be with consent for a time, that ye may give yourselves to fasting and prayer; and come together again, **that satan tempt you not for your incontinency.**

And again we are warned in Proverbs 5:15 "Drink waters out of thine own cistern, and running waters out of thine own well." Proverbs 5:20 . . . and why wilt thou, my son, be ravaged with the strange woman, and embrace the bosom of a stranger? For the ways of man are before the eyes of the Lord, and He pondereth all his goings.

Likewise in the Gospels we are cautioned that adultery does not consist in just the very physical act, it is conceived when one looks after another to lust and desire to make that individual one's own. This is covetousness pure and simple. It is at that point that adultery has been conceived, committed in the heart. Matthew 5:28.

CASE A. ABRAM, SARAI AND HAGAR

Despite the fact that Abraham (Abram) was seeking to please Sarah (Sarai) by trying to fulfill her desire to have a child by sleeping with her maid Hagar, it was still adultery. Hagar may have been her maid, but she was not Abraham's wife.

The depravity of the sin is seen in Genesis 16:2. There Sarai openly acknowledges: see now, *the Lord has restrained me* from bearing children. Please, go into my maid; perhaps I shall bear children by her. It is satan's 'I will' of Isaiah 14 with a new dress on. Abram heeded the voice of Sarai. Now that's just plain bad business. If indeed she believed, and indeed she did, that God was restraining her from bearing, how dare she pull an override to do that which He apparently did not intend at that time! It does not matter whether what she said about God was true, what matters is that she is willing to rebel against it if it is.

Hagar did indeed bear a son, his name was Ishmael. A truck load of trouble ensued from the birth of this child and continues until this day. Ishmael was not the child of promise, the child born at the directive of God from Sarah's own womb, Isaac, was the child of promise. Because of the sin committed, Ishmael was and still is a thorn in the flesh of Isaac. What is going on in the Middle East, Iraq, Iran, and Palestine is a result of this centuries old conflict and rivalry between these two brothers. See generally, Genesis 16-21.

CASE B. DAVID, BATHSHEBA & URIAH

Most of us know the story about David's fall. He was minding his own business in the palace in II Samuel Chapter 11 when he got up from his bed and walked on the roof. His eyes met the devastatingly beautiful Bathsheba bathing across the way. He made inquiries about her, determined that she was the wife of Uriah, the Hittite, sent for and slept with her.

She returned to her own house but when her husband came in from the war he sat at the king's door. King David ordered him to go and wash his feet, return to his house and sent a gift of food after him. Nice after adultery to send a thank you basket to the unwitting husband. A consolation prize for a presumably duped husband. However, Uriah sat outside of his door and would not go into his wife. No palming that pregnancy off on him!

His wife conceived by King David. In order to masque the sin, David had Joab, the commander of the army, set Uriah in the forefront of the hottest battle and to retreat from him that he might be struck down and die. No matter how you dress it up, it was a murder in the making. Uriah did die. David had the nerve to tell Joab "do not let this thing displease you for this war devours one as well as another." See what a great fire a little matter kindleth? He was the king. It was just a minor inconvenience. What a change of heart from the shepherd boy!

Immediately after Bathsheba ceased mourning for Uriah, David sent for her and she became his wife. David might have told Joab not to be displeased; but certainly what he had done displeased the Lord. The Lord sent word by Nathan the prophet that because of what David had done the sword would never depart from his house and it didn't.

Additionally God stated, that He would raise up adversity (an adversary) from David's own house that would take his wives before his own eyes and give them to his neighbors and that would live with his wives in the sight of the sun. What David had done in secret, God was going to cause to be exposed in HD, High Definition.

Although David repented of his sin of adultery, God took the life of the child after it was delivered. Fast and pray as David might lying on the ground, God's justice ensued. See, generally, II Samuel 11-12. He was subsequently blessed with a son, Solomon, who was actually allowed to build God a house in lieu of King David. II Chronicles 2.

Abraham may not have engineered his sin like David did, but he was certainly a willing participant. Adultery is bred of the lust of the eyes, the flesh, and the pride of life. We always want something, whatever or whoever it is, that we cannot or should not have.

CASE C. JOSEPH, POTIPHAR & HIS WIFE

The situation that arose between Joseph and Potiphar's wife is a prime example of this sword cutting the other way. Genesis 39. Joseph as we well know, had been sold into slavery by his brothers. He was sold out because of their jealousy and envy over his coat of many colors, his dreams of being superior and blessed of God, their being in subjection to him. His brothers took the tunic of many colors killed a kid of the goats and dipped the tunic in the blood taking it to the father to indicate that Joseph was dead. What hardened hearts!

The Midianites sold him to Potiphar. He was eventually placed in charge of all that Potiphar had. As the word of God indicates, the Lord was with Joseph and he was a successful man, just as he had dreamed. The Lord made all that Joseph did to prosper.

It is all right to prosper, but beware: there is always some evil eye eyeballing your success, poised to pounce and bring you down. In this instance, it was Potiphar's wife. Joseph was handsome in form and appearance according to verse seven. Potiphar's wife cast longing eyes on Joseph, and she said, 'Lie with me.' Joseph, who knew that the ruler had trusted everything that he had into his hands, wasn't about to cross the line by touching his wife. He did not fall asleep at the wheel like satan and presume that the throne and all of its appurtenants had suddenly become his!

We have all heard that hell hath no fury like a woman's scorn, and Joseph tasted the edge of her sword, commonly known as the bitter tongue. Despite the fact that he stated: 'How then can I do this great wickedness, and sin against God?', Mrs. Potiphar would not leave him alone. Joseph had an early sense of community and what his relationship to the Most High was. He knew that he was not his own.

She was in hot pursuit of Joseph, so much so that she plagued him with her desires on a daily basis. On one particular day opportunity knocked. There were no other witnesses present. She took advantage of the situation, caught Joseph by his garment, saying once again 'lie with me.' Instead, he fled, leaving his garment in her hand. Correct move, but a slick woman. She called to the menservants saying that her husband had brought a Hebrew to mock them. She falsely accused Joseph of attempting to rape her, his efforts only thwarted by her outcry.

Potiphar's anger was aroused and he cast Joseph into prison. Query, had he really believed his wife he would have killed Joseph instantly?! God being the good God that He is, however, gave Joseph favor with the keeper of the prison. He may not always deliver us out of our circumstances, but He will certainly be with us in the midst of them. Amen to that fiery furnace and lions' den. The whale's belly still gives me the willies though.

The word of God tells us that godliness with contentment is great gain. When one reaches out to grab more than God intends, it inevitably leads to failure. We saw this with Sarai and in every other situation in the Bible, as well as life. People want to reach out and touch that which they know is not their own. It was David's sin with Bathsheba, despite his all-consuming love of God, that led to his downhill electric slide. From the point that he committed that sin all hell began to break loose in his life. Yes, David you still have the favor of God; but your decision-making became flawed, your former resoluteness is limp:

Proverbs 6:23-29:

. . . . to keep thee from the evil woman, from the flattery of the tongue of a strange woman. Lust not after her beauty in thine heart, neither let her take thee with her eyelids. For by means of a whorish woman a man is brought to a piece of bread: and the adulteress will hunt for the precious life. Can a man take fire in his bosom, and his clothes not be burned? *Can one go upon hot coals and his feet not be burned?* So is he that goes with and to his neighbor's wife, whosoever touches her shall not be innocent.

David continued to take on additional wives, making babies by them all except Michal. He created unnecessary problems and wreaked havoc in his own life. He did not spend sufficient time chastening and guiding his children. This led to his ultimate demise.

D. MODERN DAY DIGGITY, NO DOUBT

Adultery like anything else is a tricky sin. It certainly starts out 'on the money', 'cheatin' in the next room' as an old blues song (Bobby Rush) states. Perhaps it is the secrecy, deception, manipulation and chicanery that makes it so enthralling? (Who's Making Love to Your Old Lady by Johnny Taylor). There definitely have been a multitude of songs about the very act. For example me and Mrs. Jones by Billy Paul, Ain't No Sense In Going Home Jodi's Got Your Girl and Gone, and many other songs by Millie Jackson, B.B. King, Bobby Blue Bland, Luther Vandross, Teddy Pendergrass and the list goes on.

America glorifies adultery more than any other sin. The soap operas, the internet, the magazines tout it. Marriages are made and broken on a daily basis. Marriages are no longer sacred and undertaken in the sight of God. They are made on the basis of financial need, sexual need, power plays, political liasons and connections, networking, and companionship. No doubt God is appalled. The new credo appears not to be what God has joined together let no man put asunder. Rather, if you don't like it, file, and leave it. It's just as simple as that. No thought is given to the broken vows. See the discussion on covenant breakers in Chapter 9.

On the other hand, due to modern contrivances such as cell phones, pagers, iPods, I pads, the capacity to mask actual numbers by utilization of the Internet, burn phones (use up the minutes and toss the phone) the ability to commit the sin has gained increasing facility. But God is not mocked.

It is time to tell the truth and shame the devil. Ladies we got a raw deal in the Old Testament on the issue of adultery (see discussion below) because we certainly don't commit it alone, but we do more than our fair share of fostering it.

Let's start at the home. Hubby goes off to work. You're left there seemingly tired, cleaning up, performing the typical household chores until you're certain that he is down the road. Off to the phone you go, to have phone sex with your tip. Oh it starts off innocent enough discussing the weekend, the family, mutual friends, the weather and other commonalities. Then slowly but surely it lapses into forbidden territory. A comment about the sky traipses off into a discussion about romance. A conversation about the children lapses into a discussion of what it might have been like had the two of you had children together. That conversation trails off into what it would be like to have conjugal visits and so on.

Next offense. You have become astute at (sexting) texting. You know how to say what you want to say, when you want to say it, in as sexy a manner as you can say it, replete with recent photographs, perhaps even some of the négligée that you're still wearing. Unwise indeed you are, in laying this trap, because where there is a text there is a traceable trail.

And we all know about the back door offense. The husband is kissed off to work, the children are dropped off at school, and Leroy comes in the back door before the hinges even cool off. For those who are a little more financially-endowed, Jodi meets you prior to lunch, or even during lunch at the country club, the spa, the mall, the single friend's house, the apartment or condo that you never bothered to sell before you got married, the Four Seasons or the local sleazebag hotel, motel, holiday in.

Shall we continue? How was he picked up? Was it that side glance and the whip of your hair, the leg shot as you sat like a cowgirl, the cross-legged whiplash with the spike heel dangling from your toes as you rock your leg back and forth and the poor unwitting soul into oblivion, the nylon adjustment with your foot on the edge of the chair of the desk with your fifteen year old daughter's skirt on, the oops drop of papers in the hallway and full bodybend as he passes by and asks 'lemme help', the smoothing of the hip portion of your skirt as you glance askance at him to see if he takes the bait offered, the can you help me to my car as you shamefully flirt getting strapped in. The list goes on and you know, we do reap what we sow!

I learned my lesson on this issue as a practicing lawyer. God blessed me to get my law degree and according to my colleagues, divorce cases were a quick side hustle for those tied to firms or government entities with no outside practice or no conflict clauses. Yet, whoever divorces except for the cause of adultery causes those who split to commit adultery.

Not giving it another moment's thought, I began to do 'no contest divorces'. That is, until one day I was sitting in my office and heard THE ULTIMATE CONTESTER: God asked me 'what you doing?' I responded with 'what do you mean?' He said 'what are you doing handling divorces?' Dumb me responded 'I am only doing those where the people agree they can't get along and I'm not even going into court.' He said 'yes, but you are violating my proscriptions. I said and I meant that what I have joined together let no man put asunder.' And that was the end of my quick side earnings. By the way, did I mention the fact that I was also clergy at that time as well. As the O'Jays state, Money, Money, Money, Money. God did not stop there. Since money had become my ruling passion, He cut it even more. The State Bar allowed lawyers to charge 40% plus costs for litigation, God made me cut my fee to 25% without costs. Lesson well learned.

God says **"what about thou shalt not don't you understand"**? Deuteronomy 5:18. Leviticus 20:10 made adultery punishable by death. As aforementioned, a salient feature of adultery is the fact that it focuses on the woman when we know that it takes two to tangle:

Proverbs 5:3-13:

For the lips of a strange woman drop as a honeycomb and her mouth is smoother than oil. But her end is bitter as wormwood, sharp as a two-edged sword. Her feet go down to death, her steps take hold on hell. Lest thou shouldest ponder the path of life, her ways are movable, that thou canst not know them. Hear me now therefore, O ye children, and depart not from the words of my mouth. Remove thy way far from her, and, come not nigh the door of her house. Lest thou give thine honor unto others, and thy years unto the cruel; Lest strangers be filled with thy wealth; and thy labors be in the house of a stranger; and thou mourn at the last when thy flesh and thy body are consumed, and say, how have I hated instruction and my heart despised reproof; And have not obeyed the voice of my teachers, nor inclined mine ear to them that instructed me!

Seriously, for those toying with the thought, adultery is NO JOKE. The word is clear, a man will lose his strength, his wealth, will be brought low to a morsel of bread and strangers will gather his wealth. Whew! It ain't worth it.!!!

As demonstrated above, adultery ensnares the simple Proverbs 7:6-23, will bring a man to poverty Proverbs 6:26; increases transgressions or propensity to sin, Proverbs 23:27, 20 produces moral compromise II Corinthians 12:21, causes widespread corruption Hosea 4:1-3 and will eventually land one in hell Proverbs 7:27, Revelations 21:8.

Recall John 8:1-11 that when the men brought the woman caught in adultery, Jesus stated he who is without sin cast the first stone at her. Death was permitted by stoning for the sin of adultery. I often relish the fact that He stooped and began to write in the ground. I can only imagine that He may have written I Am that I Am, or perhaps something about forgiveness and all having sinned or maybe even the name of the perpetrator, the individual with whom she'd slept.

Wouldn't it have been a marvelous thing that He scratched several (or even all) of their names in the dust. There is the ring of truth in some of this, because they got up and left from the eldest to the youngest. Whether it was out of guilt, or the recognition of who He was, they left her alone.

In I Corinthians 5:1-13 and 6:9-10 we are made painfully aware that adultery requires exclusion not only from Christian fellowship but ultimately from God's Kingdom. Take heed ye that think ye stand lest ye fall.

E. SPIRITUAL ADULTERY

Adultery is not just physical as in the cases cited above, it is also spiritual. We as God's children, as his Bride, purchased by the blood of the Lamb, have played the harlot in committing adultery against God with the very things He created and gave us dominion over. Remember from the Dedication page scriptures, the same jewels that describe the translucent All Powerful God and Bridegroom, adorn the Bride, the heavenly city, the New Jerusalem. We are ONE FLESH.

As if that is not enough, we then create things using His elements, to worship something other than Him. (eg., the molten calf Aaron created while Moses was on the mount with God). This spiritual adultery is manifested as the true essence of the relationship between the prophet Hosea and his wife Gomer. Hosea 1:1-3; James 4:4; Judges 2: 11, 17. The ultimate degradation in spiritual adultery is the decline into false teaching. Revelations 2:14, 15, 20-22.

It is a fearful thing to fall into the hands of the Living God. Get right with God.

CHAPTER 6

FORNICATION: LOVE THE ONE YOU'RE WITH

1 Corinthians 6:9-20:

> Do you not know that the unrighteous will not inherit the kingdom of God? Do not be deceived. neither fornicators, nor idolaters, nor adulterers, nor homosexuals, nor sodomites, nor thieves, nor covetous, nor drunkards, nor revilers, nor extortioners, will inherit the kingdom of God. And such were some of you. But you were washed, but you were sanctified, but you were justified in the name of the Lord Jesus and by the Spirit of God. All things are lawful for me, but all things are not helpful. All things are lawful for me, but I will not be brought under the power of any. Foods for the stomach and the stomach for foods, but God will destroy both it and them. Now the body is not for sexual immorality, but for the Lord, and the Lord for body. And God both raised up the Lord and will also raise us up by His power. Do you know that your bodies are members of Christ? Shall I then take the members of Christ and make them members of a harlot? Certainly not! Or do you not know that he who is joined to a harlot is one body with her? For "The two", He says, "shall become one flesh." But he who is joined to the Lord is one spirit with Him. Flee sexual immorality. Every sin that a man does is outside the body, but he who commits sexual immorality sins against his own body. Or do you not know that your body is the temple of the Holy Spirit who is in you, whom you have from God, and you are not your own? For you were bought at a price; therefore glorify God in your body and in your spirit which are God's.

The key to this entire discussion is the very fact that you are not your own. Joseph knew this. Because you are not your own, you have to glorify God in your body because your body is the temple of the Holy Ghost. As such you are one flesh with God, as the Bride being adorned and prepared for the Bridegroom. See Revelations 4: 1-3; Revelations 21-22 for the description of the throne of the King and the practically parallel jeweled adornment of the Bride further cementing the fact that they are indeed one flesh.

Contrary to popular belief, the categorical sin for all sexual immorality is fornication. In point of fact adultery and idolatry are subcategories of the sin of fornication. Fornication comes from the Greek the word *'porneia'*, which rivets the mind immediately to pornography. Porneia includes adultery, incest, idolatry, harlotry, and the overall concept of indulging in unlawful lust. You see that the concept is much broader than premarital sex or sleeping around.

Porneia or fornication would therefore characterize the conduct of Amon, David's son in violating his half-sister Tamar, the sister of Absalom. II Samuel 14:27. The sin consists in taking that which is not one's own and utilizing it in a way that's contrary to the proprietary interest of God himself. As the above scripture states ye have been bought with a price therefore glorify God in your body which is His.

In America and throughout this New Age generation, there is this notion of ownership of oneself, and unmitigated right to do what you want, with whomever you want, whenever you want and no one dares say you nay. The idea of sanctification, possessing one's vessel to the glory of God, is not quite the mindset of the majority of his generation. No doubt that's why we have a plethora of new disease markers, chlamydia, pelvic inflammatory disease, HIV, aids, human papilloma virus and so on. The more flagrant and defiant this society becomes, the greater the curse incurred. Deuteronomy 26-28. God keeps His promises, both positive and the negative.

The depths of the tragedy to which fornication can lead is seen in the tragic story of Genesis 34 where Dinah is violated by Shechem, the son of Hamor, who is a Hivite. Shechem took Dinah and had sex with her. He loved her and asked his father to procure her. His father went to Jacob and asked for her hand on behalf of his son as well as offering to share the land, share commerce, intermarry and provide whatever Jacob desired as a dowry and gift. vv. 7-12.

The sons of Jacob were indignant and were not willing to be appeased by the offer of marriage. Their sister had been violated, their family shamed, they were not about to be bought off. In fact in Judges the 20th chapter when the Levite's concubine was violated by the men of Gibeon who surrounded the house intending to kill him but ravishing her to the point of death, the Levite took the concubine's body, cut it into pieces and sent it throughout Israel because of his outrage.

Jacob's sons had the same rancor towards Shechem. Genesis 34:14 they agreed to allow their sister Dinah to marry Shechem only if Shechem were circumcised as required by the law. They also agreed that they would take the daughters of the Hivites to wife as he had requested. Hamor took word back to his people, happy that the matter was apparently resolved in his favor and commanded that all the men be circumcised like the Israelites.

The motivation behind this, just like Shechem forcing himself upon Dinah, was sheer covetousness. In verse 23 the statement is made "will not their livestock, their property, and every animal of theirs be ours. Only let us consent to them, and they will dwell with us." It was all about the Benjamins (denarii).

Once the men of the city were circumcised, Jacob's sons Simeon and Levi, took their swords and killed all the males belonging to Hamor. Due to their circumcision, they were too weak to fight back. Simeon and Levi flipped the script. They plundered the city. They took all of their wealth. They captured all of their little ones and their wives and plundered everything that was in their houses for the violation of their sister Dinah. vv. 25-29.

As stated earlier, fornication is a broad category with adultery, idolatry, lewdness, lasciviousness and all other sexual issues being subsections so to speak of the larger picture or hierarchy.

The woman at the well kind of straddles the categorical fence in John chapter 4. She is a Samaritan woman. Technically at least, the Jews have no dealings with the Samaritans. Yet, we find Jesus here as usual doing what no one else would do. Jesus encounters the Samaritan woman at the well at Sychar which belonged to Jacob.

A discussion ensued about water and Jesus eventually told her that he had a well of water that would spring up into everlasting life. If she drank of the water which He had she would never thirst again. He told her to go and get her husband. She responded that she had no husband. He told her that she had five husbands and the one that she had now was not her husband. In other words among the shacking, so-called marriages and fornicating, she was guilty of adultery because she had been divorced before probably for reasons other than infidelity.

Whatever the nomenclature utilized, it is clear that a throne has been set up in the life of the individual that is contrary to the edicts from the throne of God. So, what is it gonna be? Or, is the question rather, WHO?! Who do you love? Do you want him or do you really want ME, God says?

CHAPTER 7

HIGH CHAIR KISSIN' COUSINS (CO-SINS)

God intends for His people to be blessed. However, they have sought out many inventions. Recall, the 'hewn cisterns' that can hold no water? Psalms 132 states, I will abundantly bless her provision; I will satisfy her poor with bread. I will also clothe her priests with salvation and her saints will shout aloud for joy. All of this, however, is contingent upon us going into his tabernacle and worshipping at his footstool.

When we are obedient to His word, He will keep his promise. What is that promise? That the Lord has sworn in truth to David, He will not turn from it; I will set upon your throne the fruit of your body. If your sons will keep My covenant and My testimony which I shall teach them, their sons also shall sit upon your throne forever more. The obedience to My covenant and My testimony is tied to the 'sons' submission to the authority of Christ. It is actually fulfilled in Jesus, who took the throne of His father David. We attain the promise though salvation, receiving the redemption through His blood.

God intends for us to be happy, fulfilled, and satisfied. With all this goodness directed towards us, it is incredible that we erect these 'high chair kissin' cousin co-sins'. These things are delineated in Galatians 5 as uncleanness, licentiousness, and idolatry; Romans 1:26 leaving the natural use of the woman, burning towards one another, committing unrighteousness and sexual immorality; Revelations 22:15 dogs, sexually immoral, idolatry.

All of these are called kissing cousin, co-sins because they are co-sins, part and parcel of the same category of fornication. Uncleanness is a Greek word _**'akatharsia'**_. It will include all uncleanness, lewdness, incontinence, unnatural affection committed alone or in concert. When we think of the word catharsis, it connotes a cleansing or purging of oneself, 'akatharsis' is the opposite.

Licentiousness refers to sexual conduct without boundaries. It's cousin licentiousness stems from the Greek word _**'aselgeia'**_ meaning wantonness, readiness for all pleasure, no restraints, capriciousness, unmanageable forwardness, wastefulness and riotous excess. In this crew we might find the hedonists, the Epicureans, and of course the Nicolaitans.

When we step across the aisle, we encounter less and less boundaries insofaras sexual conduct is concerned. Less boundaries from man's perspective, but serious misconduct by heavenly standards.

As the word indicates in Romans 1:26 men leaving the natural use of women burned towards one another committing all unrighteousness and sexual immorality. This is modern day defilement better known as homosexuality and lesbianism. This conduct, like witchcraft finds its resting place in hell absent a repentant heart. Again, God said it, I believe that, that settles it whether we like it or not.

Revelations 22:15 refers to the dogs, whoremongers and idolaters, amongst others. They are decreed to be without. The term connotes outside, out of doors without or strange. It can also denote crushing, crumbling, beating into pieces, bruising, grinding into dust or powder. One cannot help but think about Isaiah 63 where the indignant Lord is trodding the wine press alone.

Dogs are those that are without, outside of the kingdom of God like the virgins who left to get oil and came back and the door was shut. The term is even stronger when you call to mind that the Canaanite woman came to Jesus because her daughter was demon possessed. She worshipped Jesus, but He told her "It is not good to take the children's bread and throw it to the little dogs." She asked for the crumbs that fall from the table. Jesus said that because of her faith, 'Let it be to you as you desire.' Matthew 15:21-28. So, the dogs are the unsaved folk, those outside of the covenant of promise through the shed blood of Christ. Therefore, as you continue to read, there is hope if you accept the umbrella of Jesus Christ and come in from the rain!

Whoremonger stems from the word *'pornos'*, a close cousin to or derivative of 'porneia' discussed earlier and *'pernemi'* which means to sell, a male prostitute, a debauchee, libertine or fornicator. The emphasis here is upon *'piprasko'*, meaning to traverse, to traffic, to travel, to dispose of as merchandise or into slavery. Hence the common terminology 'slave to our passions'.

Finally, we discussed a term idolatry. In the Greek the term is *'eidoloatres'* meaning servant or worshipper of that which is false. The most egregious instance I can think of is when Moses was up on the mount with God receiving the Ten Commandments. While he was up there, the people said they did not know what had become of him so they took all of their jewels and made a molten calf. When God sent Moses down because of the clamor and tumult, Aaron said the people threw their gold into the fire and 'the calf jumped out.' He said "This is your god, O Israel, that bought you out of the land of Egypt". Aaron was the one who built the altar! Exodus 32:1-4. Whew! A lightning bolt should have followed that one, but GOD IS MERCIFUL!

And, as if history does not repeat itself, Jereboam did the same thing, only he built two golden calves, setting one in Bethel, and one in Dan, proclaiming "Here are your gods, O Israel, which brought you up from the land of Egypt." I Kings 12:25-30.

Numerous instances of this kissing cousins, co-sins, are in the Bible. We are all very highly familiar with Lot, Sodom and Gomorrah. Lot had guests. The men of the town pressed against the door demanding that they be brought out 'that they may KNOW them.' In the alternative, Lot offered up his own daughters, with the added inducement that they were virgins! We discover later that they have husbands that did not leave with them. Either Lot lied or they were espoused but not consummated. To add insult to injury, Lot slept with his daughters resulting in his grandchildren being his children as well. Instead of Lot being the covering to which his name intimates, he was more like an exposé. See generally Genesis 13-19. We won't even talk about Noah's naked drunken stupor that his son Ham took delight in thereby incurring a curse for poor Canaan, the grandson. Genesis 9:20-27.

The same sexual excesses and lack of boundaries is evident in Judah who was sneaking around seeing a harlot, had sex with her, gave her his bracelets or amulet as a token. His widowed daughter-in-law subsequently gives birth to twins. He intends to kill her for her infidelity only to discover that he is the father of his own grandchildren and his bracelet was the uncontroverted proof that he had been with her. Genesis 38.

King Abimelech is also an offender in this regard. He sought Rebecca, paid handsomely for her, only to discover her sporting with her husband Isaac. It was Isaac's cowardice and Abimilech's greed that led to God closing the wombs of Abimelech's female citizens. Genesis 26:1-11. The fruit does not fall far from the tree. The same situation occurred with Abraham where he tried to pass off Sarah as his sister. Genesis 20:1-18.

The Bible is replete with instances of grievous sexual conduct. In Nehemiah 13, Eliashib the priest was in charge of the store rooms in God's house and prepared a room for Tobias where the new wine, the offerings and the oil, frankincense and holy articles were kept. Pagan women were being married and causing the men to err from the commandments of God. Nehemiah said: did not Solomon king of Israel sin by these things? Yet among many nations there was no king like him, who was beloved of his God; and God made him king over all Israel. Nevertheless pagan women caused even him to sin. Nehemiah began to run them out, pull their beards, rebuff them for dishonoring God.

We need to take a serious look at the rave parties, the hazing, the inductions into sororities, fraternities and some so-called church rituals involving orgies to enforce secrecy and loyalty, wife swapping, swinging couples, utilization of the Old Testament lifestyles and African rituals to justify polygamy. Man has his devices.

God knows and sees them. Man up and admit that it is lust, sexual perversion and quit trying to hide behind history and tradition.

Though we may be saved with all of the promises of God at our disposal, none of this will avail us in the "Situation Room" in the last and final days if we don't bear in our hearts that holiness becometh thine house. Remember that the four and twenty elders do not cease to cry out "holy, holy, holy" before the throne. Revelations 4.

Zechariah 14:20-21:

> In that day HOLINESS TO THE LORD shall be engraved on the bells of the horses. The pots of the Lord's house shall be like the bowls before the altar. Yes, every pot in Jerusalem and Judah shall be holiness to the Lord of Hosts. Everyone who sacrifices shall come and take them and cook in them. In that day there shall no longer be a Canaanite in the house of the Lord of Hosts.

CHAPTER 8

DISRUPTION, DIVISION AND CONTAINMENT

This chapter deals with the 'have it your way and it's not Burger King' 'my way or the highway' sins. Our God has a tremendous sense of humor and drew my mind to the Big Bad Wolf who said that he would huff and puff and blow the house of the three little pigs down. Well, the fact of the matter is that in the modern version, the three little pigs are destroying their own crib. The wolf is just a casual observer.

Matthew 7:24-27:

> Therefore, whoever hears these sayings of Mine, and does them, I will liken him to a wise man who built his house on the rock: and the rains descended, the floods came, and the winds blew and beat on that house; and it did not fall, for it was founded on the rock. Now everyone who hears these sayings of Mine and does not do them, will be like a foolish man who built his house on the sand: and the rain descended, the floods came, and the winds blew and beat on that house; and it fell. And great was the fall.

We know that the Rock is Jesus, the head, the capstone, the chief cornerstone coming forth with cries of 'grace, grace unto it.' Peter said 'Thou art the Christ, the Son of the Living (not dead) God. Christ said "Upon this rock (verity, truth) I will build my church and the gates of hell shall not prevail against it. **Shall not** He says, *but it is a totally different story if you open the door and welcome the calamity in!*

Christ is the foundation I Corinthians 3:11-end, and we need to be careful how we build upon Him. Worthless stuff, wood, hay, stubble or precious things? Which will you choose? The house stands strong. It *looks good in both* the wise and the foolish until inclement weather sets in**! When trials, tribulations, persecution, distress, the adversary cuts up, then you know how good your foundation really is.**

When we speak about the wise and the foolish that certainly does draw your mind back to the virgin parable(Matthew 25:1-13) the five that were wise that had enough oil to sustain them until the bridegroom came, as opposed to the other five, who were foolish, ran out and were consequently shut out. The principle in both instances is the same. He that endures until the end shall be saved.

In so far as inclement weather is concerned we are not that upset when it rains. Rain puts a damper on things but it's not that destructive, just inconvenient. However when the rains mount to the point of becoming a flood or start out with high winds in disastrous proportions such as the tsunami then it's time to 'batten down the hatches'. Floods, tornadoes, hurricanes, carry the threat of certain upheaval, the washing away of structures as well as individuals. Just think of the filth and contamination that are washed up as well. They may also carry spiritual connotation as in circumstances surrounding divorces, loss of businesses, depletion in finances, a sudden change in the stock market, death of a central figure in the family such as the matriarch and so forth. The inference is that the deluge is so strong, the current so forceful, that one has to a hold on in order to survive. Indeed, hold to God's unchanging hand and build your hope on things eternal.

Although you may tell the storm to pass, it has to come by in order to do so. And though you may sing the storm is passing over, certainly others will arise in the course of your life time. You may be able to handle the winds when they blow, but when they actually beat upon that house, you can envision the shingles coming apart on the roof, the shutters becoming tattered about the windows, the rain gutters separating from the roof of the house, the patio furniture in disarray, the sun umbrella becomes inverted, the fabric rips away from the frame while heading towards the neighbor's property. We've all been there when things come unglued. On a spiritual level, it's the same when we become emotionally undone, our faith waivers and it does not appear that our souls are still anchored in the Lord.

The word says great is the fall of the house. The word is '***Pipto***". It means to fall, perish, be destroyed, fail, fall into sin and a state of disfavor with God, to fall into judgment and be condemned or punished. This is exactly what we are talking about when we discuss the various sins that become enthroned in our hearts. They will eventually cause us to fall, to perish to be destroyed. There is that breaking away from the truth as it is in Christ Jesus, that will cause us to decline into judgment, to be condemned to be punished, despite the fact that Jesus loves us and the Bible tells us so.

A. EROS: ERRANT SPIRITS

These dismantling sins, cause disruption, division and containment. As stated hereinabove, the entire objective is to supplant the established order of God. The next aspiration is to place oneself in a position of authority to contravene the command of God. In instances where the desire for greatness is uncontrollable and all-consuming, the next step often times is to teach others to do likewise, to create clones.

The first one is idolatry. It is a broad all inclusive category of sin that encompasses all of the sexual issues in the last chapter. It rears its head here again because it constitutes replacing the will of God with something else. It is no longer Thy kingdom come, Thy will be done on earth as it is in heaven. Rather it is it's my thing I'll do what I wanna do or I did it my way. Idolatry, as stated above, is ***'eidoloatreia'***, which is image worship. We discussed this with Aaron and Jeroboam's molten calves among other things. It also conjures up the veracity of Paul's sermon on Mars Hill about them building altars to an unknown God. Acts 17:16-34.

Next on the runway is witchcraft or sorcery. It is an abomination to God. Surprisingly, the Greek word for sorcery is ***'pharmakos'***. It means a druggist, witchcraft, a magician, or poisonor. The description of poisonor appears to be more apt in light of the fact that it poisons the spirit, creating a distaste for the things of God and makes one hunger and cling to those things which cause spiritual malnutrition, alienation and . . . are detrimental. In the long run they are not just detrimental they are damning.

Deuteronomy 18 chronicles the list of things that are forbidden for Christians to practice. The Word states:

When thou art come into the land which Lord thy God giveth thee, thou shalt not learn to do after the abominations of those nations. There shall not be found among you anyone that maketh his son or his daughter to pass through the fire, or that useth divination, or an observer of times, or an enchanter or a witch. Or a charmer, or a consulter with familiar spirits, or a wizard, or a necromancer. ***For all that do these things are an abomination*** unto the Lord; and because of these abominations the Lord thy God doth drive them out from before thee. Thou shalt be perfect with the Lord thy God. For these nations which thou shalt possess, hearkened to observers of times and unto diviners: but as for thee, the Lord thy God hath not suffered thee to do so.

Passing through the fire, is ***'Abar'***. It means to cross over, passover, penetrate, to pass along, to travel, to pass away, to disappear, to transgress, to depart, to impregnate . . . Specifically it connotes the violation of a covenant, such as that the Israelites possessed with God.

Covenant breaking is dealt with in Chapter 9.

The Hebrew word for divination is **'*Quechem*'** (TOO CLOSE TO QUACKERY NOT TO NOTICE). It means witchcraft, the occult, a lying vision, self-deceit or fortune-telling. It is an effort to determine the will of the gods in order to manipulate circumstances. It is a controlling or containing spirit. Those who utilize it see no harm in steering things since they believe that they know what is best, right, good.

Diviners offer sacrifices to their gods on an altar and speak to the spirits of the dead through a hole in the ground. They shake their arrows, consult with household gods, or even examine the livers of dead animals. All of the corpses on and along the highways and streets are not roadkill. They refuse to submit to the sovereignty of God and would rather participate with soothsayers.

The observer of times and seasons is pretty simple. It's like the scripture where they look at the sky and try to determine when the Lord is coming back when the word of God says no man knows the day nor the hour. It's taking the things of nature and trying to make divine predictions based upon those things, rather than hearing directly from God.

Next on the runway to hell, it is the enchanter. The Hebrew word is **'*nachash*'**, meaning to practice sorcery, to take omens, to divine, to foretell, to prognosticate, to whisper, to hiss, to cast a spell.

The witch follows, **'*kashaph*'**. This entails the worship of idols, to use songs of magic, the magical word or incantations, to enchant, to practice magic or to use witchcraft. The combination of this and the former probably include the 'pigeon dropper' who overcomes the will and resistance of the subject and cleans their bank account like a military mess hall.

The charmer steps out on the runway next. As the name implies, it is extremely deceitful. Although it means a community, a company, a society—it carries the flavor of uniting or tying a magic knot in order to cast a spell. The Hebrew term in this **'*cheber*'**.

All of the foregoing abominable practices remind one of the showdown between Elijah and the Jezebel's prophets of Baal. I Kings 18. Can you see the prophets of Baal whipping themselves, cutting themselves, rolling on the ground, and leaping on the altar. I would've given everything to have been there when Elijah mocked them and said 'cry aloud, for he is the god; either he is meditating, or he is busy, or he is on a journey, or perhaps he is sleeping and must be awakened.' I Kings 18:24-29. For lack of a better word, all of this also 'conjures up' the imagery of the showdown between Moses, Aaron, and God against Pharaoh and his magicians. Exodus 7-11.

One who consults with familiar spirits, seeks to inquire, request information, to demand, to entreat, to beg, to interrogate is **'*Sha al*** or ***sha el*'**. The bottom line is that the individual is seeking information that either God has refused to reveal or hidden from them in particular. It is the same familiar line that Woman crossed in eating the fruit—desirable to make one wise. Genesis 2-3.

Once again we come across a wizard, *'Yidd oniy'*. It means knowing source, magician, wizard, prophesying spirit, fortune teller, familiar spirit. It is occult. God condemns those who consult wizards who peep . . .

Finally we have the necromancer. Last, but certainly not least, in the list of abominable practices. The Hebrew word *'muwth'*, the peg Canaanites use this name as the name of their god of death. She ruled over the netherworld, a place of slime and filth. There was a battle with Baal, the god of fertility. The Canaanites practice rituals that were strictly forbidden to the sons of Israel including the sacrifice of their own children.

Necromancer denotes death, withering, the chain, killing, slain or execution. This one is quite like the one above where sacrifices were made in order to read the livers. In any event it's twisted and sick and rightfully banded by God.

Which leads to the question, why is this group of sins involving alternative worship methodology classified here with the sins of disruption division and containment? At first glance, it just appears that an individual may resort to these practices on a personal level and there's 'no harm no foul' to anyone else. That is not true however. These are all seducing spirits, that seek to supplant the worship of God, which must be done in spirit and in truth. A little leaven leaveneth the whole lump. It is true that one bad apple, one bad banana, one overipe fig, one soft tomatoe or potato will eventually cause the loss of them all. And so it is in the body of Christ we are all joined together and fitly compacted by that which each joint—love-supplies, with Christ at the head. If an unclean spirit, such as those referenced above, is allowed to linger, he will eventually infest the entire group.

In retrospect the sexual sins are an effort to satiate the appetite. The categorical spiritual abominations seem to have their roots in the desire to know more than God allows, to control another human being or a situation. Hence the term containment. The driving force behind this need for knowledge that God does not supply is the need to be in charge, to control, to set parameters to one's own liking either in a community, a family, a church or other setting.

No distinction is made when it comes to the things of God. The objective is control and as far as the individuals practicing these crafts, the church is not exempt. In point of fact the church is the prime target because it is the place where the Holy Spirit is leading and guiding people into all truth. Those who practice these crafts definitely do not want the Holy Spirit to be in charge, they want control. To that end, they do not hesitate to enter into churches, become active, become officers, befriending the clergy, particularly the pastor and his or her family so that they can plant or embed their hook as deeply as possible.

Once they have obtained the favor of the congregation, they will rapidly begin to surreptitiously and viciously undermine the authority of the pastor. Should this methodology take too long, perhaps because the pastor is spiritually strong, they will move up the hierarchy falsely accusing the pastor, to elders and others waiting for the opportunity to take control. As far as they are concerned nothing is sacred and church is fair game.

You may have seen them before and not been aware what you're dealing with. They come on very strong and very friendly, very spiritual at first. However if you watch them carefully you will observe them casting a jaundiced eye at whoever appears to be well-liked and helpful to the congregation. They will begin to be obstreperous, moving contrary to the will of the pastor and his or her vision, setting motions and votes at odds and even causing decisions to be tabled for further research.

The fact of the matter is they want to bring the pastor's program and credibility to a screeching halt. They are overly concerned about the finances of the church while not tithing at all. Every inquiry that they make is about the structure of the church, the documentation relating to the structure, its incorporation, title and ownership of buildings and vehicles and account balances. Why you ask, because they are looking for a new lair for their coven. Why start your own when you can undermine something that's already in place, that is their motto. See Carnivorous Christianity in Kingdom Seed by this author.

They are in the house like Absalom, they are sons and daughters, but they intend only to have it all for themselves. They don't even attempt to fake an interest in the well-being of the congregation. Like Satan in Isaiah 14, it's all about them. They are not worried about a day of reckoning, because they cloak all of their wickedness with scriptural lavender. It soothes, it comforts. It's just the scent and that is short-lived.

B. CONSTRUCTION DEFECTS

This next crew is guilty of doing the wrong thing in the wrong way. To cut to the chase they are the hell raisers in the church. They are hatred, variance, emulations, wrath, strife, seditions, heresies and envyings. Hatred of course is obvious, it is a distinct distaste or displeasure for anything that goes against your grain which is a nice way of saying anything that you don't like.

Notice, this also carries the definition to quarrel, a wrangling, contentions, debate or strife. *'Epis eris'* seems to connote contention. Better is a dry morsel on the rooftop than to be in a house with a contentious woman so sayeth Proverbs. There are people like them in the church. They whip the church into a frenzy until everyone has a spiritual nosebleed.

Emulations is a little different. Instead of tearing things down the emulator creates a false sense of security and a false balance by propping someone or something higher than they should be. We see this in the scripture talking about Paul and Apollos. Paul said that he thanked God that he baptized none of them. The scripture further states who was Paul and who is Apollos? Paul planted, Apollos watered and God provided the increase. We are warned that if any should boast, let them boast in the Lord.

The Greek word here is *'zelos'*. It is like *'phthonos'* which signifies envy as opposed to honorable emulation and imitation. In this negative sense, the individual is grieved because s/he is a 'have not'. The individual is keenly aware of the deficiency in him or herself. This leads to a downward depressive spiral and troubling of the other in order to diminish their effectiveness. This entire process is replete with negativity and a root of bitterness. Jealousy is certainly on the throne in the situation. Sister competition may be in the house as well.

Wrath is on center stage in this talent show was well. It's probably standing right next to hatred and variance. It is defined as moving impetuously like the air or the wind only the motion is violent, passionate and indignant. The Greek word is *'thumos'*. The most blatant example of wrath would be the way that Cain slew Abel. Abel's offering was accepted by God. Cain was told that he could do better next time and would be praised for it. Rather than accept a chastening, Cain confronted his brother in the field, killed him and obviously attempted to hide the crime by burying the corpse. God however heard the cry of the blood from the earth. Having created man, he deemed that the life is in the blood. This, of course, is why we had to be redeemed by the blood of the lamb. Leviticus 17:11

Strife, is what it says it is. It is striving, struggling, seeking the preeminence on an issue or in a given situation. The battle is about control. My mind goes back to the days when we played king of the mountain. Someone would be atop a car or a boulder or some other edifice while the others would run, push, shove do whatever was necessary to unseat the victor and claim the throne as one's own. We see this sin manifesting itself when Aaron and Miriam determine that they knew more about how the cow ate the cabbage than Moses did. After all what did Moses know. He was younger. They made sacrifices to save and raise him. He stuttered. He made excuses. He had disobeyed God and married an Ethiopian. Somehow they thought that this malfeasance on Moses part rolled out the red carpet and registered them at the throne. Not so says the Lord and Miriam became a leper. Numbers 12:1-10.

Sedition takes center stage now. It means a separate faction. It connotes an opposing side. Separate being *'dicha'* and the faction being *'stasis'* hence the word *'dichostasia'*, a negative spin on dichotomy, which means to stand separately. Unfortunately there will be differences in the body of Christ and at one point in the ministry Paul and John Mark went their separate ways. Acts, though the crowning birth of Christianity, also saw a lot of division, suspicion and distrust amongst the apostles. Each one questioning the validity of the other, their stance on particular issues such as eating things offered to idols, fornication and circumcision, and their trustworthiness in situations where God would call upon one to seek out and assist the other. No one trusted Saul who became Paul.

The next bad actor/malefactor is heresy or ***'haireomai'***. It means to remove, take away or to loose presumably from one's moorings, to hold in suspense, or to take up a yoke as a burden. Loosing appears to be the more apt description in this classification of sin in light of the fact that one is drawn away from scriptural doctrine to itching ears that will not endure sound doctrine.

The Bible talks about those who heap to themselves teachers after their own liking. We see this in the New Age movement, and the efforts to establish gay and lesbian churches when in fact God intends that they repent and be saved. A church can no more be established by calling itself one when it's conduct is contrary to the word of God than a marriage can be made by two people coming together of the same sex. This is in line with rotating known adulterous, molesting, womanizing, fornicating pastors rather than calling them to task.

Yes, Yes, people can worship whenever, wherever and however they want. It's a free world, with free speech but you can't call it a church. Yes, people can unite with whoever they want, whenever they want; but it is not a marriage as defined by God. As the word of God says you shall know the truth and the truth shall make you free. You cannot take a round peg and put it into a square hole.

God has a clearly defined order for everything in His word. None of us are privileged either to add to or subtract from it that's the bottom line. And it is this second group of sins, seeking to masquerade as the word of God, that seeks to disrupt or discredit the word or cause division in the house, Unlike the class A eros: errant group involving witchcraft etc. this group practices containment as well, they just do it on the sly. They are astute at playing the game, they know their goal and they will do battle with anyone that gets in their way.

We see this strife, the variance, the divisions, emulations in some of the old-line churches where there's the one group that's committed to tradition, the high hymns and anthems, and the other group that wants to try new things, such as praise dancing, miming, gospel rap and the like.

C. THE ROWDIES

The final group are the bad boys. These are the rabble-rousers, the ones who like a good stiff drink, a wild party and then they back up with the A group and start all over again. They consume a great deal in riotous living. They are reckless and often callous and indifferent to the feelings and well-being of others. The chief end is to have a good time and they don't see why everybody else is on their case. This group consists of the murderers, drunkenness, revelings, and liars.

Satan is the father of all of this rebellion against God. Jesus calls him the father of lies. In John 8:44 Jesus stated" You are of your father the devil, and the desires of your father you want to do. He was a murderer from the beginning, and does not stand in the truth, because there is no truth in him. When he speaks a lie, he speaks from his own resources, for he is a liar and the father of it."

So there you have it. Jesus said that satan was a murderer from the beginning and we see that because he killed the communal spirit that was between Adam, Woman and God. Adam was created in the image and the likeness of God. God stated "Let US make man in Our image and in Our likeness. Man was made out of the dust of the earth and God breathed in him and he became a living soul. Woman was made out of the side of man and therefore of the same composition.

They lost their ability to commune with God as a result of their rebellion against the known will of God with regard to the tree of the knowledge of good and evil. See generally Genesis 2-3.

The murderous spirit resurfaces in the homicide involving Cain and Abel. From another perspective, the murderer from the beginning appellation may very well refer to Lucifer's efforts to supplant the Most High God. When you think about it there is absolutely no way that he would have been able to accomplish this coup d'état without trying to take God out, a virtual impossibility. When you think about it, you see just how treacherous and ridiculous Lucifer's plan was. As I've stated before, he must have had way too much angel dust.

This sin of reveling is derived from the word 'Kosmos'. Cosmus is the god of feasting and reveling. His rituals included drunkenness, feasting, impurity, obscenity, excessive drinking and banqueting. Part of the festal company would eventually become engaged in obscenity and sexual orgies of the grossest kind. So when you consider things like the word cosmopolitan and the fact that not too long ago some of the youngsters consider themselves Kosmos but they were really referring to drunkenness, debauchery and reveling.

All of the foregoing are thrones in one's life contrary to the known will of God. The only way back to God is to empty the throne, to deny oneself all of these sensual and political 'pleasures' and entanglements, and return to the only true God.

Jesus is King of Kings and Lord of Lords or nothing at all. In other words, He will not be second chair to anyone or anything.

CHAPTER 9

SELF-PROMOTION / SELF AGGRANDIZEMENT

Although this last category of throne craving sins really covers the entire gamut, the title was reserved for this last group because they are particularly heinous. It involves a temperament that will do 'anything' to win. These demons are cutthroat, underhanded, supplanters, that know no boundaries.

The notables in this group include malignity, whisperers, backbiters, haters of God, despiteful, proud, boasters, inventors of evil things, disobedient to parents, covenant breakers, implacable, unmerciful. These sins differ from the others because the others are the kinds of sins that one could arguably fall into without even being aware until it's too late. In other words the other groups could entail innocent blunders. Not so with this group. This group is deliberate, malicious, self-willed and Godless. In fact, one could go so far as to say that this will be the composition of the group that has the nerve to set itself up to fight against Christ upon his coming again. Considering Lucifer's musical inclination, if this group had to be characterized in another fashion, they would be depicted as Satan's Symphony. Close perusal of these sins reads like a Who's Who of the violators of the 10 Commandments.

Malignity, is **_kakoetheia_** connoting that which is evil and customary. It means ill nature and entails negatively interpreting the conduct and actions of others in an evil fashion. It sounds like the twin of 'evil surmising'. It is vicious, malevolent, acting out, the externalization of an evil habit of mind, attributing the worst evil motives to others. It is a cancer, which if left unchecked, will destroy the other good cells and tissue.

The scriptural personage that bears the closest resemblance to malignancy would be Haman. Haman was astute at falsely accusing others of misconduct, blowing it out of proportion, and trying to get the King to kill them. The case in point is that of Mordecai. Putting others down in hopes of promoting oneself is the name of the game here.

Whisperers are malignant as well. They would be the first cousins to malignancy. To whisper means to **_psithuristes_**, to secretly slander or backbite. The first ones that come to mind in this instance would be Joseph's brothers. They hated him because their father loved him, made him a coat of many colors, and because of two dreams that he had establishing that he would be the leader of the family.

The brothers got together and discussed how to do away with Joseph. They had every intention of killing him but for Ruben and Judah. Ruben and Judah decided that he should be left in a hole or well and sold him to Midianites.

Thereafter, they ripped up the coat of many colors, dipped it in blood returning it to their father indicating that Joseph was dead. This group of sins would also include the scribes, Pharisees, Sadducees and the hypocrites, who were busy backbiting Jesus at every turn.

Backbiters are the twins to the former two. **_'Katalalos'_** which means random, and open degradation of another without giving any thought whatsoever to the truthfulness of the accusation. Actually, the more false it is the better. The objective is the negative impact at the expense of another. They are all culpable busybodies. Judas would certainly fit this group. He sat at meat with Jesus and still sold him out for a paltry sum of money.

Haters of God are just what they say. They despise Him, and anything that relates to Him, His Son and His kingdom. These are not just reprobate, they are lawless. As Jesus stated they 'hated me without a cause.' Quite frankly they look a lot like Cain because Cain killed Abel because Abel's deeds were righteous. The religious order of the day sought the death of Jesus because he undermined what they perceived to be as their rightful position and authority. To really toast their turbans he went around healing people that heretofore had not been healed (lepers), raised the dead, cast out devils and just made them look bad.

'Hubristes' is the word for the despiteful. They are described as insolent wrongdoers. They commit a wrong for the sake of doing wrong because they want to impart pain, inflict injury and reproach upon another. These of course would be those who utilized Samson's girlfriends and wives to determine his weakness.

This might also characterize Abigail's husband, Nabal, because he refused to feed David and his men stating that he was not accustomed to feeding those who fled from their masters. Nabal was described as being churlish, refusing to help or accommodate others.

Proud is the next class. **_'Huperephanos'_** meaning to appear over. These people establish themselves above their fellow men, preferring themselves. Obviously Jacob and his conduct towards his brother Esau, in duplicity with his mother, might fit this category. Woman or Eve would be another one in light of the fact that the inducement for her to finally eat the fruit was that it was "desirable to make one wise". Clearly she thought she would be preeminent.

The conduct of Aaron and Miriam in defying Moses' authority because he married an Ethiopian woman was also motivated by their determination that because they were called, they had just as much authority as their brother Moses.

God set them straight, because He said He spoke with Moses "face-to-face". The crème de la crème of course of pride is satan himself in Isaiah 14, but this has already been addressed herein above, and extensively in Kingdom Seed in the sub book on Carnivorous Christianity.

Boasters walk hand-in-hand with the proud. Suffice it to say that the word is clear in I Corinthians 13 that love does not vaunt itself. Boaster is the word *'alazon'* in Greek. It falls in line with those that are haughty, even high-minded. The word of God states that promotion comes from the Lord. Additionally, one ought not to think more highly of himself than he ought to think. Scripturally, this would encompass the entire argument about Paul as opposed to Apollos.

Inventors of evil things would run the gamut of the malignant, whisperers, backbiters, haters of God, proud, boastful and despiteful. All of these things are done to inflate oneself at the expense of others. It is a tremendous ego trip. However, the word is clear, he who exalts himself shall be humbled,he who humbles himself shall be exalted. The first shall be last and the last shall be first. This is criminal mischief of the first order.

Disobedient to parents will not be belabored here either. Children are to obey their parents in the Lord. The ten commandments state unequivocally to honor thy father and thy mother that thy days may be long in the land which the Lord thy God giveth thee to dwell in. The word is *'apelthes'* which means that one is not only disobedient but unable to be persuaded, intractable and stubborn. David's son Absalom probably comes closest to this description.

'Asunthetos' is technically the worst of the worst from a purely spiritual standpoint. Covenant breakers are what the Israelites have always been. They had the Solaric (Genesis 1:14-), Edenic (Genesis 1:26-), Adamic (Genesis 3:14-), Cainic (Genesis 4:11-), Noahic (Genesis 8:20-), Abrahamic (Genesis 12:1-), Hagaric (Genesis 16:7-), Sarahic (Genesis 17:15-), Restorative (Exodus 15:26-), Mosiac (Exodus 20:1-), Levitic (Numbers 25:10-), Palestinian (Leviticus 26; Deuteronomy 11:8-), Salt (Leviticus 2:13-); Davidic (II Samuel 7:1-) and New (Matthew 26:28) They never complied with the terms of their end of the bargain. Let your yeah be yeah and your nay be nay. It is better to not to vow at all, than to vow and not pay. However, some vows made in haste and presumption should be broken. A prime example is Jepthah's vow to make a sacrificial offering of the first thing he saw when he came home because of the victorious military campaign. The first thing he saw was his virgin daughter running to greet him. He kept the vow and killed her! Judges 11:1-4. This is not the way that we serve God, otherwise He would have had Abraham follow through and kill Isaac.

"Aspondos" is the first cousin if not the twin to the covenant breaker. This one is described as being without libation. In other words s/he is a trucebreaker. This would definitely be Saul of Tarsus who promised 'on the regular' that he would treat David right. However, he pursued and attempted to kill him no less than 29 times. This one and the covenant breaker are definitely first cousins to the liar. We've already been told that satan is the father lies.

The final candidate is the unmerciful. God says to the merciful He will show himself merciful; but to the froward He will show himself froward. One only needs to recall the unrighteous judge who gave the woman what she requested not because he was merciful but because she kept bugging him. *'Aneleemon'* is the word for unmerciful and is defined as the failure to show compassion. This would also be the debtor who was forgiven all, and then sought one who was in debt to him and demanded to be paid in full. This is a definite double standard.

All of the sins seek by hook and crook to place the individual privy to them above everyone and everything else. Compassion is the sine qua non of Christianity. Lacking compassion is the equivalent of lacking Christ. The blueprint for Christianity is based upon compassion and love. Christ talks about being hungry, naked, homeless, thirsty and imprisoned. He also talked about taking care of the widows and the orphans. Those who do these things are fruitbearers, the others are chaff.

He summed it up in one line: If you love ME, keep My commandments. Ephesus, Do you love Him or have you left off from your first love seeking a quick fix?!

CHAPTER 10

CONCLUSION

The inspiration behind writing this has been to establish that as Isaiah says He is God and besides Him, there is no other. I have been guilty like everyone else in establishing all kinds of thrones in my life; but I've come to realize that there is only one throne and only one God. Only ONE is Worthy:

"And I saw in the right hand of him that sat on the throne a book written within and on the backside, sealed with seven seals. And I saw a strong angel proclaiming with a loud voice, who is worthy to open the book, and to loose the seals thereof? And that no man in heaven, nor in earth, neither under the earth, was able to open the book, neither to look thereon. And I wept much, because no man was found worthy to open and to read the book, neither to look thereon. And one of the elders saith unto me, weep not; behold the Lion of the tribe of Judah, the Root of David, has prevailed to open the book, and to loose the seven seals thereof. And I beheld, and, Lo, in the midst of the throne and of the four beasts, and in the midst of the elders, stood a Lamb as it had been slain, having seven horns and seven eyes, which are the seven Spirits of God sent forth into all the earth. And He came and took the book out of the right hand of Him that sat upon the throne. And when He had taken the book, the four beasts and four and twenty elders fell down before the Lamb, having every one of them harps, and golden vials full of odours, which are the prayers of saints. And they sung a new song, saying Thou art worthy to take the book, and to open the seals thereof; for Thou wast slain, and has redeemed us to God by Thy blood out of every kindred and tongue and people and nation; and hast made us unto our God kings and priests; and we shall reign on the earth. And I beheld and I heard the voice of many angels round about the throne, and the beasts, and the elders; and the number of them was ten thousands time ten thousand and thousands of thousands; saying with a loud voice, Worthy is the Lamb that was slain to receive power, and riches, and wisdom, and strength, and honor, and glory, and blessing." Revelations 5:1-12.

Yes, there should no longer be any doubt. HE IS WORTHY. There is only one Lord, one faith, one baptism, one God and Father over all, who is above all in all and through you all.

"Verily, verily, I say unto you, he who does not enter the sheepfold by the door, but climbs up some other way, the same is a thief and a robber. But he who enters by the door is the shepherd of the sheep. To Him the doorkeeper opens, and the sheep hear His voice and He calls His own sheep by name and leads them out. And when He brings out His own sheep, He goes before them; and the sheep follow Him, for they know His voice. Yet they will by no means follow a stranger, but will flee from him, for they do not know the voice of strangers . . . All whoever came before Me are thieves and robbers but the sheep did not hear them. I am the door. If anyone enters by Me, he will be saved, and will go in and out and find pasture. The thief does not come except to steal, and to kill, and to destroy. I have come that they may have life, and that they may have it more abundantly. I am the good shepherd the Good Shepherd gives His life for the sheep." John 10:1-11

The crux of the entire matter is that all of these other 'high chair wannabe thrones' are established by the one who seeks to steal kill and to destroy, none other than satan himself. He deceives you into getting involved in the various categories of sins so that he can enlarge his territory. He is very astute at his brand of delegation—helping you set yourself up as sovereign over your own life. Once you are outside of the God Hedge, you are his. Whatever turf you gain is his.

Most of us know that we don't even have the capacity to fight our way out of a paper bag. So satan doesn't **just** come out and say let me put you on the throne with the sin. No, like the sly Fox that he is, he simply leans against the light post in the shadows waiting for the unwary but curious to enter into his web. Oh yes, he offers delights all right; but what do they cost you in the long run? You have a good time; but where do you end up in the long haul?

We can set up all the junk thrones we were seduced by and bought; but it still does not amount to a hill of beans next to the only wise God, our Creator, the One who has superior title to our lives because of the shed blood of His Son, our Lord and Savior Jesus Christ.

There are many contenders for the throne but only One who is worthy and merits sitting upon it. I can't help but think of the song: King of my life I crown Thee now, Thine shall the glory be; lest I forget Thy thorn crowned brow, lead me to Calvary, lest I forget Gethsemane, lest I forget Thine agony, lest I forget Thy love for me, lead me to Calvary by Jennie E. Hussey and William J. Kikpatrick.

It Is Never Too Late! I urge you to stop what you're doing right now and pray this prayer while I touch and agree with you:

Father God I have sinned and against Thee and Thee only have I sinned. Your word says that if I confess with my mouth the Lord Jesus Christ and believe in my heart that He was raised from the dead I shall be saved. Romans 10:9. I may have given my life to you when I was younger but I took it back and did my own thing. I confess that I have set up thrones in my life that were not of your making. In I John 1:9-10 your word says that if I confess my sin, You will be faithful and just to forgive me and to cleanse me from all unrighteousness. So here I am dear Lord, pardon mine iniquity for it is great. I renounce the hidden things of darkness, dishonesty and deceit that I have been involved in. I renounce all the things of satan and his darkness and I decree myself free by the grace of the precious blood of Your Only Begotten Son from the drawing, pulling, enticing and seducing spirits, slings, arrows and the hooks of the enemy. I am no longer subject to them. I thank you O Lord God for delivering me and making me a vessel for Your use. I give You the glory in Jesus' Most Holy and Righteous Name Amen.

WELCOME HOME!!!

My final prayer for you is that you not only see Him with the eyes with which I see Him; but that you are blessed to love Him the way that I have and always will:

Ezekiel 1:26-28:

And above the firmament over their heads was the likeness of the throne, in appearance like sapphire stone; on the likeness of the throne was a likeness with the appearance of a man high above it. Also from the appearance of His waist upward I saw, as it were, the color of amber with the appearance of fire all around within it; and from the appearance of His waist and downward I saw, as it were, the appearance of fire with brightness all around. Like the appearance of a rainbow in a cloud on a rainy day, so was the appearance of the brightness all around. This was the appearance of the likeness of the glory of the Lord. So when I saw it, I fell on my face, and I heard a voice of One speaking. And He said to me, son of man, stand on your feet, and I will speak to you. Then the Spirit entered me when He spoke to me, and set me on my feet; and I heard Him who spoke to me. And He said to me: son of man, I am sending you to the children of Israel, to a rebellious nation that has rebelled against Me ; they and their fathers have transgressed against Me to this very day. For they are impudent and stubborn children. I am sending you to them, and you shall say to them, thus says the Lord God. As for them whether they hear or whether they refuse—for they are a rebellious house—yet they will know that a prophet has been among them. And you, son of man, do not be afraid of them nor be afraid of their words, though briars and thorns are with you and you dwell among scorpions; do not be afraid of their words or dismayed by their looks, though they are a rebellious house. You shall speak My words to them whether they hear or whether they refuse, for they are rebellious. But you, son of man, hear what I say to you. Do not be rebellious like that rebellious house; open your mouth and eat what I give you.

Revelations 22:11

. . . he who is unjust, let him be unjust still; he who is filthy, let him be filthy still; he who is righteous, let him be righteous still; he who is holy, let him be holy still. And behold I am coming quickly and My reward is with Me to give to everyone according to his work. v. 20 He who testifies to these things says, Surely, I am coming quickly.

Amen. Even so, come, Lord Jesus!

INSPIRATIONAL BIBLIOGRAPHY

1. Nelson's NKJV The New Open Bible 1990 Thomas Nelson Inc.

2. The Chumash, The Stone Edition Mesorah Publications 2000

3. Nelson's New Illustrated Bible Commentary 1999

4. Exegeses parallel Bible 2001

5. The New Strong's Exhaustive Concordance of the Bible

6. Dake's Annonated Bible

7. The Expositor's Study Bible

8. Halley's Bible Handbook

9. Wilson's Dictionary of Bible Types

10. A Dictionary of Scripture Proper Names by J.B. Jackson

11. The New Compact Bible Dictionary by Zondervan

12. The Hebrew-Greek Key Study Bible (KJV Baker)

13. Number in Scripture E.W. Bullinger

14. Max Lucado, The Devotional Bible NCV

Printed in the United States
By Bookmasters